Just Passing

A play

Colin and Mary Crowther

Samuel French — London
www.samuelfrench-london.co.uk

Copyright © 2008 by Colin and Mary Crowther
All Rights Reserved

JUST PASSING is fully protected under the copyright laws of the British Commonwealth, including Canada, the United States of America, and all other countries of the Copyright Union. All rights, including professional and amateur stage productions, recitation, lecturing, public reading, motion picture, radio broadcasting, television and the rights of translation into foreign languages are strictly reserved.

ISBN 978-0-573-12127-2
www.samuelfrench.co.uk
www.samuelfrench.com

FOR AMATEUR PRODUCTION ENQUIRIES

UNITED KINGDOM AND WORLD
EXCLUDING NORTH AMERICA

plays@samuelfrench.co.uk

020 7255 4302/01

Each title is subject to availability from Samuel French,
depending upon country of performance.

CAUTION: Professional and amateur producers are hereby warned that JUST PASSING is subject to a licensing fee. Publication of this play does not imply availability for performance. Both amateurs and professionals considering a production are strongly advised to apply to the appropriate agent before starting rehearsals, advertising, or booking a theatre. A licensing fee must be paid whether the title is presented for charity or gain and whether or not admission is charged.

The Professional Rights in this play are controlled by Samuel French Ltd, 24-32 Stephenson Way, London NW1 2HD.

No one shall make any changes in this title for the purpose of production. No part of this book may be reproduced, stored in a retrieval system, or transmitted in any form, by any means, now known or yet to be invented, including mechanical, electronic, photocopying, recording, videotaping, or otherwise, without the prior written permission of the publisher. No one shall upload this title, or part of this title, to any social media websites.

The right of Colin and Mary Crowther to be identified as author of this work has been asserted in accordance with Section 77 of the Copyright, Designs and Patents Act 1988.

CHARACTERS

Man, aged 40-70: serene, refreshed
Woman, aged 40-70: volatile, exhausted
Nurse, aged 50-60: worn, caring - male or female, Robin/Robyn

A park bench
Time: the present

To all those receiving care and all those caring – especially to Alan.

Further titles by the same authors, published by
Samuel French:

Footprints in the Sand (Colin Crowther)
The Lost Garden (full length)
Noah's Ark (for children)
Till We Meet Again
Tryst (Colin Crowther)

JUST PASSING

A park bench, old and weathered, clearly the favoured perch of an incontinent small bird, stands just to R of C, angled slightly to face out L

It is early one clear Spring morning, and the bench basks in dappled sunlight. It is surrounded by a little patch of low, straggling shrubbery, in which an empty sweet wrapper and a crisp packet have caught. An unloved, unvisited spot, planted, inevitably, with senecio *and* cotoneaster, *and left to get on with it*

None of this appears to bother the middle-aged Man who sits on the R end of the bench, still and comfortable, content to look out over the valley below. Only an old walking stick leaning by his side hints at an earlier illness, but it is so weathered it may well have been left out there for months: a stick which, like an old dog, is happier now waiting than walking

A Woman comes out to him from USL. *About his age, she looks worn and pale, the effect emphasized by the clothes she wears: long, flowing lines in shades of grey*

The contrast to him could not be greater. She looks carelessly elegant, he scruffily comfortable in an old cardigan, cords and, incongruously, leather indoor slippers. Whereas she looks angry, hurt and exhausted, he looks blissfully serene and reinvigorated

He seems to have been expecting her, for he smiles, but they do not feel the need to acknowledge each other, even when she sits on the stage left arm of the bench, with her back to him. Instead, she breathes very deeply. It is then, with her eyes closed, that she appears to realize he is there

Woman Thought I might find you out here.
Man Can't seem to ... drag myself away.
Woman Some of us don't have the choice. (*Rising abruptly*) I've no time for this. (*She takes her keys out from her pocket*)
Man For what?
Woman Games. (*Sitting heavily on the bench*) God, I never knew I could be so tired!
Man You're off, then.
Woman So much to do. After so much stillness, so long waiting, suddenly... How'd you know?
Man You've got your car keys out.
Woman House keys. Same ring. Came by taxi. Couldn't trust myself to... Oh God, is he waiting, too?
Man Did you pay him?
Woman No.
Man He'll wait.
Woman Poor man!
Man Rich man, soon.
Woman I seem to keep everyone waiting, these days.
Man I told you: pay the bills the day they come through.
Woman I did — I think. Except the phone bill. You wouldn't believe my phone bill!
Man I would.
Woman Oh, drat it! It can wait. He can wait. They can all dratted well wait!
Man That's the spirit!

The Woman jumps up and breaks slightly L

Woman And you can wait, too. This is my time! Mine! And I'll do what I damn well want with it!
Man Not so loud. (*Pointing, briefly, left and right*) You're enough to wake the dead
Woman Oh!

She looks up; her eyes search a building thirty feet away to her right; sees someone in a first floor window; calls out to them

Hallo...!
Man (*prompting*) John.
Woman John. How's the——?
Man Angina.
Woman —Heart? (*Pause*) Are you sure it's his heart?
Man Why?
Woman He can't hear me. His window is wide open, yet he can't hear me. (*Pause*) What am I doing here?
Man You can leave — any time you want.
Woman I can't.
Man Then stay.

The Woman seems persuaded. The Man sits back, contentedly soaking up the sunlight

There is a pause

The Woman breaks ULC *and looks* USL

Woman I can't! I should be down there. Helping. Or something.
Man You'd only be in the way.
Woman Typical!
Man Relax.
Woman How can I? It's only the tension holding me together. If I let go—for an instant—I'll go *sklwa*—like a jellyfish on a beach.
Man *Sklwa?*
Woman It's what they do. Jellyfish. On the beach.
Man *Sklwa.*
Woman Reminds me. I've forgotten something. What was it? My memory. Just doesn't seem to——
Man You should make a list. I keep telling you——
Woman Oh, you and your famous lists!
Man You and your infamous jumping in and doing things without thinking them through.

The Woman utters a low, growling scream as she comes to the back of the bench

Woman Damn! Damndamndamndamndamn, And drat!

Pause

Man I'm just saying.
Woman Will you look at this place! What a God-forsaken, scrubby, scruffy mess!
Man I like it.
Woman Oh yes! It's just the sort of mess you would like!
Man Other people like it.
Woman Who? People like you? Old men in macs?
Man People who like views. Down across the valley. Out over the town.
Woman And you all line up, do you? You and your little old men, on the crest of this hill, exposing yourselves to the view.
Man I do not have a mac.
Woman Pardon me.
Man And this is not a hill.
Woman You didn't have to climb it!
Man You came here.
Woman Looking for you.
Man Robin comes here.
Woman Looking for you.
Man I'm not sure. Sometimes I think he comes out here to get away.
Woman (*looking* USL) They're here.
Man I know.
Woman Thought I might—leave them to it.
Man Who did you use in the end?
Woman Sudbury's.
Man Good people.
Woman I hope so.
Man Trust me. I know.
Woman Yes. I suppose you would.
Man Anyway, Robin's with them.
Woman Robin?

The Man nods

Robin's wonderful.
Man Dirty sense of humour.
Woman Filthy.

Pause. They both chuckle

Stories he can tell. Things he knows. Places he must have been.
Man Makes you wonder where he spends his days off.
Woman Trust you to ruin it.
Man What have I said now?
Woman Mind like a sewer. The worst of it is you've even got me thinking like you now. You've got inside my head. (*She breaks* R, *clear of the bench*)
Man That's love for you.
Woman Marriage, anyway. Funny, we spend the first ten years trying to house train the savage beast. The next however many wondering if we wouldn't have been better off with Tarzan, after all.
Man I don't understand.
Woman You're not meant to.

The Man rises, walks forward to DSC, *unaided*

Man I do love being here.
Woman (*hopefully*) With me?

The Man is not listening, only looking

Man First time I came out here, it was dusk. Well, eventually it was dusk. Can't think how I got here. All at once, the lights came on—like the seaside—Blackpool! Strings of street lights, banks of shop lights, then house lights, one by one, as people—other people—went home and I, only I, was left behind, unlit—a child again, frightened, in the dark. Then I saw that stick—all pale and weathered—like it had been left outside—weeks—months ago—to guide another traveller through another night. When I go, I think—I think I'll leave it here, for the next little boy left alone in the dark.

The Woman shivers

Woman Wondered where it came from.
Man Then they found me—worked out how I'd got away—really tore me off a strip. They don't like one of their charges to make a run for it—not on their shift. I was confined to my room. To my chair. To my little cot. Like a naughty boy who once— almost once—escaped— what was coming to him——

He turns suddenly and faces out R

Woman Three years. Long time.
Man And now, all that has changed.

The Woman is completely abstracted, staring out over the view

Woman Nice for you.
Man Susie——
Woman Don't call me that! (*Turning towards him*) I never knew you were so fond of nature.
Man I'm not. I came here to feel connected—to feel I was still part— linked in some way—to all of that—to all of you.

The Woman crosses to RC

Woman You're not the only one, you know. I came here too.
Man I thought this was my secret place!

The Woman stops below the bench, staring at the stick

Woman Robin brought me—last week—he had—oh, something to tell me. Ever since, I've been coming every day. Whenever I wanted to really talk to you and needed you to really listen. Funny I should feel so much closer to you up here than ever I did down there.
Man I—don't remember.
Woman I'd rant and rave at you—And you'd say such—beautiful things—Always the right things.
Man Doesn't sound like me.

Woman Then I'd go back down, back inside. Find you—snoring, like as not.
Man I like a good snore.
Woman Good. You did enough of it.

Pause. The Man feels awkward, invaded

Man Isn't it time you were off?
Woman You want shot of me!
Man You said there were things—things you had to do.
Woman Oh, God, yes. I made a list. You see? There are still things you don't know about me.
Man Well, where is it?
Woman I lost it.
Man Typical! (*He breaks up to* LC)
Woman It was the only way I could get any sleep. Otherwise I lay there, and just when I was in freefall into my first decent night's sleep in three years, I'd jerk awake and think, "Oh, I must do this, first thing"; "Tuesday, remember, you've got to do that." So I kept a pad by the bed and a pen in the drawer. And the list—the blessed list under my pillow. (*She laughs*)

The Man shakes his head. The Woman stops laughing

> Only yesterday—yesterday I changed the bed and put the old sheets in the wash— Oh!

Now it's the Man's turn to laugh

> At least I tried.

Suddenly the Man hears birdsong, out front, DSL, *about eight feet off the ground. He wanders towards it*

Man There's that bird again!
Woman I don't hear it.

Man You're not listening.

The Woman sits

Woman I thought you'd gone—when I didn't find you—door closed—down there—name gone—I thought I'd missed you—door locked—locked out——
Man (*very excitedly*) Can you hear it now?

The Woman shakes her head, close to tears

Woman Help me.
Man What?
Woman Say good bye.
Man (*appearing to be totally entranced by the bird*) I just had to get out—get away from this overwhelming feeling that suddenly— I was under everyone's feet.
Woman (*panicking*) Not yet!
Man In everyone's way.
Woman (*suddenly relieved*) Oh, I do know how that feels! Always in someone's way. Always having to share you with someone else. And they never knocked—just barged in—even—that time I climbed onto your bed—for a quick cuddle—remember?—the blessed window cleaner!

The Man laughs and the Woman smiles

Man I hated that.
Woman No, you didn't. You thrived on it. You'd look up when they came in. Smile. At them. But for me? I'd be lucky if you stayed awake.
Man I depended on them.
Woman You let them do everything for you. Shower you. Touch you.
Man I needed them!
Woman I needed you!
Man (*distracted again by the bird on the tree out left*) It's a blackbird! A beautiful blackbird!

Just Passing

Woman Who cares!
Man He does. You're sitting on his bench. He comes here every day. Perches on the back of that bench. Sings his little heart out. Don't know why.
Woman (*looking at the bird lime*) Well, it's not constipation.
Man Please, don't spoil it. This could be the last time we meet. Make it special. Not long now before they move me out. (*He turns and comes towards* DSC *to look out again over the valley*)
Woman It's too soon. I'm not ready. Why can't my mind catch up! I need to make sense of this.
Man I'm just waiting for them to collect me.
Woman Waiting...
Man Just passing...
Woman Aren't we all? (*She rises and turns away*)
Man (*turning to her*) Don't go. Not yet.
Woman Still afraid of the dark?
Man I wanted to visit, one last time, places, people I loved.
Woman And that meant here?
Man And you.

The Woman joins the Man, slipping her arm through his

I love it, just here. The mist snaking through the valley. Trees tearing at the sky. And the sun tipping every branch and twig green with envy.
Woman Spring... You're changing... Used to be so taciturn—only spoke in grumps and humphs. Most of the time you never spoke at all.
Man Strong, silent type.
Woman No. More the mumbling, muttering type.
Man Oh, I don't think——
Woman ——The dog talked more than you did. And he's been dead three years! The goldfish——
Man ——You do exaggerate!
Woman That's what conversation is. Making something out of nothing, out of life's little nothings.

The Man shrugs

Blowing it up big so you can see it up close, more clearly.

The Man is clearly stumped

The Woman is getting more exasperated

Because Life, Truth, IT lies in what people say. The little details. The small print! Where are we? Why are we here? Where are we going? The answer, the answer is in the things people say!
Man Why bother?

The Woman withdraws her hand and turns to face the Man

Woman (*at screaming pitch*) Why? Because words are all we have! Conversation! Real or... Oh, if you don't know, I'm not going to tell you!
Man Ha!

The Woman puts a hand tenderly on the Man's arm

Woman We talk to reach out to someone else—for reassurance that we're not alone.
Man We *are* alone.

The Woman gives up, withdraws her arm, breaks up to LC

Except for...

The Woman turns, intrigued

The Man points L

The Woman scans a building off L. *Second floor: no one. First floor: no one. Ground floor: there she sees*

Woman Oh. Mrs Lamb.
Man Anderton.
Woman Lamb. Good morning. Lovely day. How's — life? I must pop in to see her later.

Just Passing

Man Another time.
Woman Bring some flowers.
Man She likes carnations.
Woman I'll remember.
Man (*lovingly*) You'll forget.
Woman (*with awful realization*) She can't see me. I've been worn away to a shadow of my former self. Whereas you——
Man Never felt better.
Woman All day I've had this feeling ... I'm not really here. No one can see me, hear me ...
Man Mmm?
Woman What did I just say?
Man Something ... very interesting.
Woman Nice try.
Man My God, there's an edge to your voice these days.
Woman Who's sharpened it?
Man (*smiling*) But you love me really?
Woman I'm glad you think so.
Man Say it.
Woman (*pointedly*) After you. (*Pause*) Sorry. (*Pause*) Oh, why is it always me? Why do I always feel so guilty? Last night, I laughed—something—oh, I don't know —I laughed and immediately I thought, "Sh! Hope no one heard me!" As if I—but only I—have no right to be happy. Only guilty.
Man It's all right.

The Woman breaks to below the bench

Woman No, it's not! (*Pause*) Other people live and laugh and just get on with it. Me? These days I can't do anything without thinking about it—causes—consequences—and whichever way I turn I find myself—guilty. I think of all the unhappy people who should be happy. Which makes me so sad I can't laugh. Which makes me so angry I can't feel sad. Which makes me——
Man —An idiot!——
Woman —Guilty.

The Woman sits. Pause. She rises

I must go. That poor taxi driver... See? Guilty, milud, and I want four hundred and sixty three other offences taken into account!

The Man breaks up to left of bench

Man He'll wait. They'll all wait.
Woman No I'm the one who waits. All this time I've waited. Expecting the call. When I get it—I've not—I'm not—ready...
Man It's not your fault.
Woman It is! All this time I've wanted more time—to do my own thing. Now... I've got the time... And no "thing" to do with it... (*She sits R of bench*)
Man I understand.
Woman No, you don't! I do wish you'd stop saying that! You never used to. What's come over you?

The Man sits on the left arm of bench

Man I used to think I'd look forward to the day you'd retire and I'd have you home all day—to talk to. But, if you were home all day... we'd have nothing to talk about. Now I think perhaps we need some time apart so when we do meet again, we'll have something to...
Woman Idiot!
Man Guilty... But what I mean is I do so understand.
Woman That's the most patronizing thing—to think you know how someone else feels.
Man Right.
Woman Say something else.
Man There, there.
Woman There, there? (*Rising*) Is that all you can say? There ruddy there?
Man I just thought——
Woman There you go again—making me feel selfish and mean and bad-tempered and so blinking tired—oh no, and now so guilty!

Pause

Just Passing

Man Please. I hate it when you cry.
Woman Well, you needn't worry. I'm not. These aren't tears. Not real tears. Because for every tear there's a—— Will you look at my nails! (*Now she cries real tears and then breaks* RC)
Man It's only natural.
Woman It is?
Man You're a woman.
Woman You bugger! You selfish, mean, bad-tempered——
Man That's better!
Woman You want real tears? I'll give you real tears!

Suddenly the Man hears something or someone calling him from USL. *He rises and turns towards the call*

The Woman steps toward him

   Don't go!
Man They're ready for me.
Woman Oh, that's nice! Now you're free, free as—as a——
Man Blackbird.
Woman —free to fly off, wherever you like. And I'm the one who's tied down, shut indoors, put aside.
Man I've served my time.
Woman And I've just started mine!

The Woman sits, C *of the bench, then turns away to touch the Man's discarded walking-stick*

The Man half-looks USL, *impatient to be off*

   Where will you go?

The Man shrugs

   Don't you care?
Man Pastures new.
Woman And that's it?

Man Does it matter? I'll go where I'm sent.
Woman Oh, that's typical of you! No spark. No fight. No spine.
Man No. It broke.

The Woman tries to shrug this off and get back to something she feels safe with: her anger

Woman Why would you never listen? Never read? Never follow instructions? Why didn't you look where you were going?
Man It was an accident.
Woman Flat-pack wardrobes?
Man Old lady.
Woman Setting up the computer?
Man Not her fault.
Woman Asking directions?
Man She had a stroke. At the wheel. Hit me side on. An accident!

The Woman is desperate now to get back to that old, familiar anger

Woman Have you forgotten Weston-super-Mare?
Man For goodness sake!
Woman "I know a shortcut," says he. "Through this field". What happened?
Man I broke my spine.
Woman Next thing we know, a tank comes over the rise.
Man Ended up in hospital.
Woman An armoured tank!
Man Then carted off here.
Woman We were on the army firing range!
Man Four years!
Woman And look at what you're wearing! Men used to be such peacocks. Now you all look like something a peacock sat on.
Man Looks don't matter.
Woman Then what does?

Pause. Change key. The Man turns to face USR

Man I wanted to change the world.

Woman What happened?
Man The world changed me.
Woman Still, you made your mark.
Man More like a smudge. A sticky finger-print.
Woman And me?
Man You succeeded. You made your mark. On me.

The Woman is pleased

The Man comes to stand behind her

> Where will you go? After the nail-dresser, the hair-dresser, the shops for more clothes? You bought an entire new wardrobe last week. It must be worn out by now.

The Woman shakes her head

Woman I need new shoes. And a new handbag. That old one's a disgrace.

The Man smiles. The Woman will be all right now

Man What's for dinner?
Woman I don't know. Hadn't thought that far. *Scallopine alla Milanese*?
Man Your cooking's improved.
Woman There's a new Italian round the corner—with liquid brown eyes.
Man All right. Then I'll have—let me see—roast beef, Yorkshire pud, all the trimmings.
Woman In your dreams.

He breaks R

Man I love dreams. I've lived in them for three years. Dreams are a wonderful mistress, a terrible master. (*His head jerks suddenly towards* USL)

The Woman does not even bother to look up. She knows

Woman They're ready. (*She rises*)
Man Yes.
Woman I ought to be there, helping them pack. Oh—the suitcase! Oh, finnan haddock! Finnan haddock, finnan haddock, finnan haddock... Fishcakes!

The Woman sits SR of bench and sags

The Man perches on the opposite arm of the bench

Man You're gorgeous!
Woman Now he tells me!
Man I couldn't before. Couldn't move, couldn't speak. Remember?
Woman Four years ago. Year in hospital. Three years in this place. Three years I've been coming here.
Man Never missed a day.
Woman Well, for a wife, a husband isn't just a hobby, he's a full-time occupation. Oh, don't interrupt. Strangers at first. Had to get to know each other all over again. This time with me making all the moves.
Man I tried my best.
Woman Sharing... I'm not sure what now——
Man The view... The moment...
Woman —And now, after all this time, you were going to leave me. Without a word!
Man Ah.
Woman After all we've been to each other. For sixteen years.
Man Seventeen. We lived together a year first, remember——
Woman Shut up. Leaving me behind!

The Man sits beside the Woman, trying to see it from her point of view

When Robin phoned, I thought—I know it's stupid—I thought: you could at least have phoned yourself.
Man Now that is stupid.
Woman I know.

Just Passing

Man I wasn't expecting it.
Woman I was!

Pause

Man How?
Woman Robin told me. Last week. He brought me out here. I'd never been before. And told me. In the midst of this ... desolation.
Man Then what the hell are you fussing about, woman?
Woman Please don't swear. (*Pause*) And don't call me woman. (*Pause*) When he called this morning—so early—I thought—At last. I can sleep. A decent night's sleep. Then I thought: I must do this, then I must do that. I must have a shower and wash my hair. I could have it cut. Tinted. Start all over again. I'll spring-clean. And the garden. Haven't done the garden for years. I'll get a man in. I'll get a firm in. I'll have it landscaped. I'll get a job. Have a holiday. Go away. To the sea. I'll sell up. I'll sell up and move to the seaside. I shall paddle. Naked. In slippers. With pom-poms. Little pink pom-poms.
Man And what did you do?
Woman I fell asleep, dreaming of pom-poms, hundreds and hundreds of little pink pom-poms.
Man But you hate pink.
Woman I know! When I woke—I felt refreshed—and angry—so angry—and guilty—and late. I was so late! Which made me guilty. Which made me angry. Which made me exhausted, all over again. Over and over again. (*Pause*) How was it for you?
Man (*shrugging*) All right

The Woman rises and breaks c

Woman Oh, for once!
Man You could come with me?

Pause while she drinks in the implications of this

Woman You sod! You selfish little sod! You'd like that, wouldn't you? Have me follow you to the end of the earth? From work to hospital,

hospital here, here to— God knows where! The answer's no. My life's here. My garden. My hobbies.
Man You hate the garden. You have no hobbies. No life to speak of.
Woman And whose fault is that? Who's eaten up all my time? Oh, Simone was right. I've driven myself into an early grave for you.
Man Ah, Simone! Might know she'd——
Woman —I've given you the best years of my life. Oh, God! I sound like my mother! You utter, frigging bastard!
Man I give up! My fault. Must be. I'm ... sorry—sorry I——
Woman —Typical. Claiming the moral high ground.
Man What now?
Woman *I* wanted to say sorry. *I* wanted to be the one to say thank you and——
Man —Good bye?
Woman Yes.

Pause

Man I just want to see you happy.
Woman Don't say that!
Man Then what do you want me to say? Tell me! I'll say whatever it takes to make you——
Woman (*turning on the Man*) I only ever wanted to hear you say one thing: to hear you say you love me.
Man But I do!
Woman But you never said it!
Man I must have done.

The Woman shakes her head

I felt it.
Woman I know you felt it. But you never said it. You joked it. Called it over your shoulder. Over the phone even. Signed your name to it on a soppy card. But you never said it. To my face. And meant it... And now, I shall just have to live with knowing you never will. (*She returns to the bench and sits*)

Just Passing

The Man shrugs

Man I love you.
Woman Too late! Too late.

The Man gives up and looks out over the valley

Man I woke, about half past four, and the world had changed. I wondered why I'd woken up; what had changed. And then I heard. A single bird, a blackbird, sensing the first hint of light, had begun to sing, enticing the sun to draw closer, closer. Purple gave way to pink. More birds sang—pleading, cajoling—till dawn relented and smiled on the world and their song—their song shredded me. Tore the light out of me—gold out of pink—and I could feel my whole body tingling with joy and life and a new beginning—dying to find the words to ask: this light is their life, their joy, but me? What to me is dear as this? And I thought of here. And you. Suddenly, I could walk and talk again. But I didn't need to. I could fly—no, I could swim through the air— Suddenly— I was here. Then you were here. At last I was whole, complete — And now I can sing like my blackbird for the sheer happy, helpless, bursting joy of it all! (*Pause*) I love you, Susie. You're the surge in my tide. The sap in my forest. You raise my twisted arms to the light and tip me green and gold with splendour. You're my hope, my joy, my promise of a new start to every day. You're my Spring.

Pause

Woman Well, that's all right then... I just wish you'd told me.
Man I wish I'd done a lot of things. Climbed the Eiger. Fought the good fight. Gone on safari.
Woman Lake Garda, That's where I wanted to go.
Man You still can.
Woman Not the same. Without you.
Man But I'm saying——
Woman —I know what you're saying!

Man You're in a terrible mood.
Woman Must have been welling up inside me. Like one of those geysers. In New Zealand.
Man Somewhere else I never went.

The Woman starts fishing in her pocket for a clean tissue

Why do you never have a tissue when you need one!

The Woman pulls out a folded piece of paper

Woman Oh, look. I found that list.
Man What does it say?
Woman Get up. Shower. Wash hair. Phone Simone.

The Woman screws it up and throws it away

The Man places his hand on the Woman's

The Woman looks at him directly

Man Time to go.
Woman I don't want to go.

Enter a Nurse USL, *or at least someone wearing what is, but not quite, a nurse's uniform*

There's something about it, apart from the ink-stained top pocket, bulging side pockets and scuffed shoes, that points to a more casual, idiosyncratic approach to a less urgent situation than a hospital

Nurse (*calling out from a distance*) Thought I might find you out here.
Man (*standing*) Robin! Good to see you!
Woman Can't seem to ... drag myself away.
Nurse Just came to say ... good bye.
Man Thank you. (*He starts to move to* C)
Woman Sorry.
Nurse Oh, and to give you a message. If I can find it.

Just Passing 21

The Nurse stops when he reaches c. As he fishes in one pocket for a pile of little messages, each from an identical little pad, each in his meticulous hand, and begins to work through them, we can see how tired he is, coming to the end of a long week of early shifts but only halfway through one of those mornings with too much happening, too much to remember and already the feeling that it's all slipping away. Time to retire? Or just to have that long overdue break? Perhaps because he is so tired, he only ever seems to see the Woman, never to quite acknowledge the Man. But perhaps we are reading too much into it: like any good nurse, he deals with us all, but one at a time

Woman Felt I was under everyone's feet back there.
Nurse Know the feeling. Why I come up here myself. Get away for a while. So...
Man Robin, you look...
Nurse —How're you feeling now?
Man —Exhausted.
Woman Can't remember feeling so tired. Been sitting here—in a dream—half an hour. If you hadn't come...
Nurse I can go away again?
Woman Better ... leaving them to it.
Nurse Quite right. (*He fishes in his other pocket and brings out an unopened packet of cigarettes. He stares at it*)
Man Wish you'd never started?
Nurse Wish I'd never stopped. (*He stuffs them away – business first – then bottles out*) Love that view.
Woman Yes.
Nurse (*coming forward to look at it more closely*) They've been now. Been and gone.
Woman Oh ... good.
Nurse Twelve years this place has been open. Twelve years I've been coming up here to get away from the non-stop ringing of telephones, call buzzers, shouts of "Robin, will you do this?" and "Robin, where's that?"
Woman A lot of people depend on you.
Nurse And I love it. Wouldn't have it any other way. Just...sometimes I need to get away... Thank heaven in twelve years, no one's worked

out where. No one on the staff, anyway.
Man But we all know—
Nurse *(to his left)* Morning, Mrs. Lamb. *(To his right)* John. All right? They all know, bless 'em, all know my little secret, and I know theirs. They never tell. Nor do I.
Man Because we love you.
Woman True. We all love you.
Nurse Never thought of that. Felt it, sometimes. But no one ever says it. Know what I mean?
Woman Oh, yes!

The Nurse begins a wide circle upstage of the bench, looking at it, thinking about it

Nurse So many people get drawn here. Lovers meeting. Lovers parting. Seen it all this bench has. Heard it all, too. On a summer's night——
Woman I thought I'd come, one last time, visit the places he—we loved.

The Nurse comes to the back of the bench and leans over it

Nurse Thing about a view, it lends perspective. Down there the valley: timeless, getting on with it, as it always has, always will. Out there the town: monument to human greed and busyness, no more substantial than a gravestone.
Man Looks pretty solid to me.
Nurse Two hundred years old at most. The valley? Two hundred thousand. I like a bit of geography.
Man "God made the country and man made the town", eh?

The Nurse recognises the quotation, but for the moment can't quite place it

Woman Oh, Robin——
Man The more you look, the more you listen, the less things are the way you thought...

Woman How come, when you're on your own, everything takes half the time, but there's twice the time to do it in?

The Man and the Nurse both shrug

I don't know...where to go, what to do.
Nurse (*inspiration striking*) Cowper! (*Pointing out* L) See that?
Man The old mill?
Woman Browning's?
Nurse (*pointing out* R) And that? With the cupola?
Woman The library.
Nurse What links the two?

The Man and the Woman are both stumped

In the library, just as you go in, there's a bust.
Woman William Cowper.
Nurse Pronounced Cooper. The poet. Seventeen-thirty-one to eighteen-hundred.
Man "God moves in a mysterious way, his wonders to perform."
Woman Oh! He lived here?
Nurse No. But our William Cowper did. Born here, eighteen-forty-two. In the workhouse. And was given the name—the workhouse Master being fond of a bit of literature—of our English poet.
Man "He plants his footsteps in the sea,
 And rides upon the storm."
Woman So that's William Cowper.
Nurse Apprenticed at twelve to the mill, owned by—
Man Robert Browning.
Nurse Another workhouse graduate. Rose to be manager. Then—and here's my point—donated part of his considerable wealth to fund the town library.
Man The point being——?
Nurse What to do. With your life. Look around. Examples galore. Live for others. Like William Cowper. Or go there. (*He points straight ahead*)
Woman St. Barnabas'?
Nurse Halfway down the nave. Left-hand side. Brass plaque. "To

the memory of Elizabeth Galway, relict of this parish". Buried two husbands. Lived in the Manor House. Left two pence for the poor, each Michaelmas. Live for pleasure. I like a bit of local history.
Woman Message?
Nurse That was it.
Woman You said you had a message for me?
Man There's that bird again.
Woman Skylark.

The Nurse follows the sound and comes slowly back to centre, looking in its direction

Nurse Song thrush. Britain's favourite little chorister.
Man He's off.
Nurse Sings from March to July. Extensive repertoire. Up to one hundred musical phrases, each one repeated three or four times, and always——
Man Robin——
Nurse And this is interesting—always sings from the same spot: a prominent post, small tree, bush——
Woman Or park bench.
Nurse Possibly. I like a bit of wildlife. So. Next question. Where to go.
Woman Pastures new.
Nurse Good for you.
Woman And you?
Nurse Oh, I'll stay. Serve out my time here.
Man How do you cope, Robin?
Nurse I keep my body busy, my mind active. Key to health however old you are.
Man How?
Nurse When people come here, they're defeated. Ashamed. They've given up. They feel they've lost their home, family, future. Like your husband, after that terrible car accident.
Man He's right.
Nurse My job—to help them feel that here they fit, they belong, they're accepted— on their terms. And always try to welcome their loved ones as part of this family too.

Just Passing

Man "Ye fearful saints, fresh courage take,
   The clouds ye so much dread
   Are big with mercy, and shall break
   In blessings on your head."
Woman And if that doesn't work?
Nurse I push them out here. Let them soak up the view. Get a new perspective.
Man And that's your secret?
Nurse No. My secret—and I should have told you this before—I pushed your husband out here one afternoon—got called in—some emergency—end of shift—went home—never gave it another thought. It was eight o'clock and well dark before they found him. Sorry.
Man So that's how I got out here, all those years ago. It was you!
Nurse My advice? To you? Take up smoking. Smoking is a wonderful excuse to stand still. No? Then take up dog-walking. Walking a dog is a wonderful excuse for getting out and meeting people. People are the answer in the end. On my dog walks I meet a local historian, two bird-watchers, a physicist, a poet, three teachers, a postman and a retired meteorologist—who was on the telly...I met my wife on a dog walk...
Man And that's your secret.
Nurse (*nodding*) The real answer to despair is to learn something new every day; meet someone new every month; and go somewhere new every year.
Woman We did have a dog, once.
Nurse There you are, then. (*He returns to his notes*) What's this one? (*He takes his spectacles out of his breast pocket to read it and in doing so finds another note. He reads the other note first. He comes down to* LC) Ah. Man from Sudbury's. Said he'll be in touch this evening.
Woman Oh, good.
Nurse And if you still want early next week, could you look to registering the death asap, only there's a build-up at the crem. On a Monday.
Woman Oh, God.
Man Thanks, Robin. Delicately put.

The Man holds the Woman's hands in his

Nurse His words not mine.
Man Was there something else?
Nurse Hate this bit.
Woman We know.
Nurse Always comes out wrong——
Man —Robin!
Nurse Sorry. Bad time. Never is a good time. Manager says: Could you look to clearing his room? No rush. You've got three days by rights. But often it's easier now. Clean sweep.
Woman Sorry. Forgot the suitcase. You did say, but... Doesn't matter. There's nothing I want here.
Nurse No worries. Nursing home can sort it out for you. Er, books to our little library. Always appreciated. Clothes to our store. Always come in handy. Toiletries to the tombola. Armchair to — whoever gets the room next? TV the same? That just leaves the painting.
Woman His favourite. Bin it.
Man Susan!
Nurse Oh, but it's beautiful! Little boats——
Man —Not boats. Barges. East coast barges, sitting low in a choppy sea——
Nurse —Bobbing about at anchor——
Man —Fully rigged, their sails of rust and cream, just waiting for the tide to turn and a favouring wind to waft them away to distant shores——
Nurse —Just chugging up and down the Thames, shouldn't wonder. Weekend sailors, eh? Still, nice colours. I like the way those ominous clouds are parting and a shaft of sunlight is breaking through——
Man —It is called *The Turn of the Tide.*
Woman Gives me the creeps.
Man No, no. Symbolic, you see, of the journey we all must——
Woman —Have it.
Nurse Oh, I couldn't!
Man (*shocked*) Don't you want it?
Nurse If you're sure?

Just Passing

Woman He would want you to have it.
Nurse Trouble is, we do have a policy on valuable gifts.
Man It's priceless!
Woman Ten pounds from a car boot sale.
Man That's not the point!
Nurse Oh, no problem there then.
Man Oh, have it, have it.
Nurse Thank you very much. Well, no rest for... (*He spots the walking stick*) Oh! — That's where that stick got to. (*He takes a step towards it*)
Man No!
Woman (*rising*) Leave it. Why not? For the next weary traveller?
Nurse Oh. OK.
Woman I'm on my way. I only came to say good bye.
Nurse I just wish they did. You care for them, sometimes for years. They never say...goodbye. Silly...tired, that's all. Daft things you think when you're tired. But in the end they all go without saying goodbye... stupid of me, but somehow I feel bereft...left behind.

The Woman crosses to the Nurse

Woman Oh, Robin!
Nurse I envy them. Pleased for them as well...but somehow can't help feeling I'm missing out.

The Woman hugs the Nurse

Still, I get to hear the birds sing. And know, one day, they'll sing for me.

The Woman kisses the Nurse on the cheek

Woman Thanks, Robin. For everything.

The Woman and the Nurse are now both embarrased

I must...go.

Nurse Perhaps as well. The taxi driver was getting restless.
Woman Taxi!
Nurse Oh! That was it! The message!
Woman Oh, God, the taxi!
Man I love you.

But in her haste, the Woman does not hear the Man, does not bother even to turn back

The Woman exits USL

Nurse Lovely woman.
Man Yes.
Nurse Lovely man.
Man (*considering this*) Thank you.
Nurse Lovely view. Ah, well. Duty calls. (*He moves off* U)
Man Think I'll stay...until the memory fades.
Nurse As one moves out another moves in.
Man In the end, we're all just passing through...

The Nurse suddenly turns and looks out L

Nurse There's that bird again.

The Nurse and the Man stay and listen as the CURTAIN *falls*

FURNITURE AND PROPERTY LIST

Further dressing may be added at the director's discretion

On stage: A park bench with bird lime on it *Leaning against it*: an old, weathered walking stick
Straggling shrubs that could include *senecio* and *cotoneaster*
Empty sweet wrapper
Crisp packet

Personal: **Woman**: a bunch of house and car keys on one fob
A folded piece of paper with a list on it
Crumpled tissues

Nurse: small, handwritten notes in one side pocket
An unopened packet of cigarettes in another side pocket
A pair of spectacles and a note in a breast pocket

LIGHTING PLOT

Property fittings required: nil
Exterior: gradually brightening to noon-light by the end of the play

To open: Dappled shafts of early morning Spring sunlight, lighting the park bench and other acting areas

EFFECTS PLOT

There are no effects in this play.

It is particularly important that no music opens or closes the play and no birdsong is heard.

www.ingramcontent.com/pod-product-compliance
Ingram Content Group UK Ltd.
Pitfield, Milton Keynes, MK11 3LW, UK
UKHW021848210426
5322IPUK00022B/544